Selfishness vs. Self-Care
WORKBOOK

We Have the Power to Create Our Lives

FINDING UNCONDITIONAL LOVE, PEACE, AND HAPPINESS

SELFISHNESS *vs.* SELF-CARE

We must be willing to take time to take care of ourselves, to learn to replenish our energy. This is not to be confused with physical energy. I believe emotional energy is more important because if we are emotionally drained then we don't have the energy to do anything… including nurture and nourish our physical selves.

When we take into consideration the effects that negative and positive energy has on our state of being, we will see our lives change once we start to put our emotional well-being first. It's from this place that we have more love, joy, and more support to offer life.

This book has been created to inspire you to take time to enjoy yourself with yourself. We must take time to relax and be… use this inspirational work book to change your state of being by making a choice to do so.

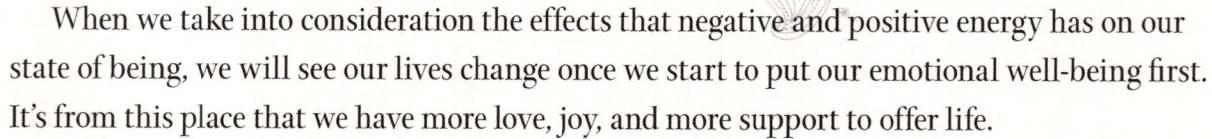

The author and those associated with her shall not be liable or responsible for any damage or injury allegedly arising from the methods, formulas or information put forth in this workbook. This workbook is a self-help and inspirational guide for personal development. We assume no responsibility for inaccuracies or omissions.

No part of this workbook may be produced commercially either by off-set printing, digital printing or on the internet without permission of the publisher.

Selfishness vs. Self-Care Workbook ©2016
by Susan Haines

smhaines1@gmail.com
www.SusanHaines.net

Design & Layout: Laura H. Couallier, Laura Herrmann Design

ISBN: 10-0997002662
First Printing

Choose to be HAPPY

We have within ourselves
the power to be happy.
Happiness is a state of being.
If we choose this state, the external
world shall reflect this truth.

In detail, what is happiness?

In great detail...
What makes you happy?

In great detail...What inspires you to happy thoughts?

What are three examples of happiness, to you?

1. _____
_____
_____
_____
_____
_____

2. _____
_____
_____
_____
_____
_____

3. _____
_____
_____
_____
_____
_____

How does it feel to be happy?

Are you a happy person?

If yes, why?

_____
_____
_____
_____
_____

If no, why not?

_____
_____
_____
_____
_____

List five people that you know are happy.

1. _____

2. _____

3. _____

4. _____

5. _____

What affects do you imagine happiness would have on your body?

CREATE YOUR STORY
...the one you wish to live.

How would your love life change if you were truly happy?

CREATE YOUR STORY
...the one you wish to live.

If you were truly happy, how would your life change?

List 10 things that you could be happy about.

1. _____
2. _____
3. _____
4. _____
5. _____
6. _____
7. _____
8. _____
9. _____
10. _____

What percentage of your day is spent thinking happy thoughts?

Who makes you happy?

Why should you choose to be happy?

Unconditional LOVE

We are pure love.
We are meant to live the best
life we can imagine, from a
place of complete fearlessness.
Anything less is not love.

List in detail four things you love about your life.

1. _____
_____
_____
_____

2. _____
_____
_____
_____
_____

3. _____
_____
_____
_____
_____

4. _____
_____
_____
_____

List five people you love, aside from your family.

1. _____

2. _____

3. _____

4. _____

5. _____

Why do you love these individuals?

Do you love yourself?

What do you love most about your body?

CREATE YOUR STORY
...the one you wish to live.

Imagine all is perfect with love as the guiding force... describe your ideal day.

If you were in love with yourself on a daily basis, what thoughts would you think?

Who do you love most in the world?

List three things you love about your career/work.

1. _____

2. _____

3. _____

Is it important to treat yourself with love?

Are your friends and family loving towards you?

Is love painful?

_____
_____
_____
_____

How do you know that you love yourself?

_____
_____
_____
_____
_____

Are you a loving person?

_____
_____
_____
_____
_____

Finding PEACE

Peace is a state of being. As we observe nature we see the seasons changing, the sun rising, the birds singing, the flowers blooming—all in a day's work. It happens without complaint, without worry, or without fear. It just is. As we should be, residing in the midst of life, just being, without concern—for life, just is.

Are you a peaceful person?

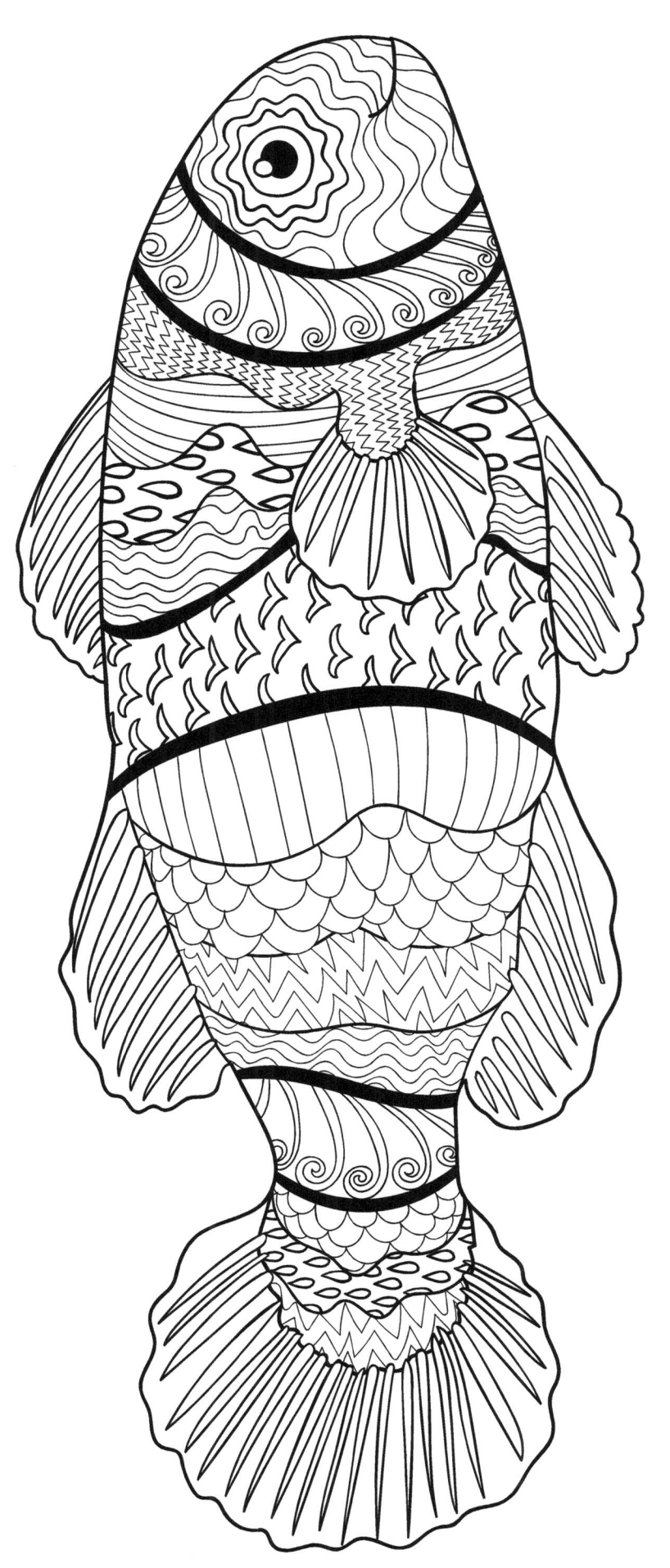

Do you look for peaceful solutions?

Do you live in a peaceful environment?

Do you work in a peaceful environment?

What does being "at peace" mean to you?

How do you create peace in your world?

List five ways you could experience more peace.

1. _____

2. _____

3. _____

4. _____

5. _____

List five people that are peaceful.

1. _____

2. _____

3. _____

4. _____

5. _____

What are five character traits you notice in a peaceful person?

1. _____

2. _____

3. _____

4. _____

5. _____

Is being peaceful a choice?

_____
_____
_____
_____
_____

If so, why is it a choice?

_____
_____
_____
_____
_____
_____

Imagine that you're at peace with life and everything in it.

What are you doing?

_____
_____
_____
_____

Where are you?

_____
_____
_____
_____

Who are you with?

_____
_____
_____
_____

Is the world a peaceful place?

If yes, why is it?

_____
_____
_____
_____
_____

If no, why isn't it?

_____
_____
_____
_____
_____